GERMANY is one of the most culturally influential European nations, as well as one of the main economic powers throughout the world.

Welcome

GERMANY
★ ★ ★

It is Central Europe's largest country, and is bordered by Denmark to the north, Poland and Czech Republic to the east, Switzerland and Austria to the south, and France, Belgium, Luxembourg, and the Netherlands to the west. It consists of a federation of 16 states that roughly correspond to regions, each having unique and distinct cultures. In this book, we will be learning about places to visit in Germany.

THERE ARE LOTS OF PLACES TO SEE IN GERMANY!

Geography Book for Children

Children's Travel Books

BABY PROFESSOR

EDUCATION KIDS

Speedy Publishing LLC

40 E. Main St. #1156

Newark, DE 19711

www.speedypublishing.com

Copyright 2017

Neuschwanstein Castle

NEUSCHWANSTEIN CASTLE

Füssen, which is an old town that is located between the Allgäu and the Ammergau Alps, known as a popular alpine resort as well as a winter sports center, is a good place to start and close to the Neuschwanstein Castle, which is one of the most well-known royal castles in Europe.

GERMANY
★ ★ ★

King Ludwig II, between 1869-86, constructed this battlement-covered fortress with several towers which was Walt Disney's inspiration for their famous castles in their theme parks.

King Ludwig II

BERLIN'S BRANDENBURG GATE

The Brandenburg Gate was built in 1791 for King Frederick William II and modeled after the Acropolis in Athens. It is located in the Mitte District of Berlin and was Berlin's original Neoclassical structure. Including the four-horse chariot which is perched at the top, this structure measures 26 meters tall.

On each side of the structure there are six large columns which form five passages: four used by regular traffic, and the center was only for the royal carriages. Two buildings located at each side are decorated with Doric columns. These buildings were once used by guards and toll collectors.

Brandenburg Gate

Undoubtedly known as the most iconic structure in Berlin, it also was, at one-time, part of the famous Berlin Wall and was symbolic of the Berlin's division between East and West for a few decades.

GERMANY
★ ★ ★

COLOGNE CATHEDRAL (KÖLNER DOM)

The Kölner Dom, the Cathedral of St. Peter and St. Mary, that towers over the Rhine is the most remarkable landmark located in Cologne. It is a masterpiece consisting of High Gothic architecture and was started in 1248 and considered to be the project that took on a tremendous amount of ambition during the Middle Ages.

Cologne Cathedral Interior

It is one of Europe's largest cathedrals. Its amazing interior covers 6,166 square meters and features 56 large pillars. The Reliquary of the Three Kings, located above the high alter, is a work of art from the 12th century that was designed by Nicholas of Verdun for storing relics of the Three Kings that were delivered from Milan.

GERMANY
★★★

In addition, you won't want to miss the panoramic views from the South Towers, the stained glass from the 12th and 13th centuries that are located in the Three Kings Chapel, as well as the Treasury that contains several precious objects.

HISTORIC PORT OF HAMBURG AND THE MINIATUR WUNDERLAND

The magnificent Miniatur Wunderland, located at the Port of Hamburg, is the largest model railway in the world, appealing to both the young and the old. With over 12,000 meters of track, this huge scale model consists of sections that are dedicated to Scandinavia and the USA and incorporates 890 trains, over 300,000 lights, as well as more than 200,000 human figures.

Some guests have been known to spend several hours exploring this amazing world with detailed miniature airports (having airplanes that actually take off), cites, rural areas, as well as busy harbors. By the way, you will also want to visit the Port of Hamburg while you are there. This huge harbor covers 100 sq. km. and is known to be the Gateway to Germany and its best to explore by boat.

Port of Hamburg

Warehouse District

You can then walk the harborside promenade which is a beautiful route for walking, and also see the Warehouse District that consists of tall brick-built warehouses in continuous lines.

GERMANY
★ ★ ★

THE BLACK FOREST

With its densely-wooded, dark hills, the gorgeous Black Forest is one of Europe's most visited regions. Located in Germany's southwest corner it is heaven for those who enjoy hiking. It descends to the Rhine towards the west and slopes gently to the upper Danube and Neckar valleys.

The Famous Waterfall at Todtnau

GERMANY
★ ★ ★

Todtnau, Germany's oldest ski area is one of the popular spots, as well as the Bad Liebenzell resort and Baden-Baden's spectacular spa facilities. Additional attractions you might want to see include the Black Forest Railway along Triberg, including the famous falls, as well as Triberg, where you will find the Black Forest Open Air Museum.

GERMANY
★ ★ ★

MUSEUM ISLAND

In Berlin, you find Museum Island, otherwise known as the world-famous Museumsinsel, which can be found between the Kupfergraben and the River Spee, which includes many of its most important and oldest museums. At this heart of the pedestrian-friendly district you will find the Old Museum which was built in 1830 to exhibit royal treasures.

BODE-MUSEUM

Museumsinsel

DER DEUTSCHEN KUNST MDCCCLXXI

National Gallery

The land located behind the museum was soon set aside for the "knowledge of antiquity" and art. The new museum took shape between the years 1843 and 1855 and in 1876, the National Gallery was added, together with the Bode Museum, that was built in 1904 as a home for antiquities collections.

The Ishtar Gate, Pergamon Museum

In addition, during this walking tour, you will find the Pergamon along with its historic buildings recreated from the Middle East. There is so much to see here, you will probably want at least two days so that you can take in all Museum Island has to offer.

ZUGSPITZE MASSIF

The Zugspitze Massif, which is part of the Wetterstein mountain range, is surrounded by deep valleys and lies between Austria and German. At 2,962 meters, the eastern summit is adorned by a gilded cross and you can reach it by taking the Bayerische Zugspitzbahn, a cable car, or a cog railway.

You might also enjoy this area aboard the Tiroler Zugspitzbahn, which is a railway that runs to the Zugspitzkamm station, located at 2,805 meters. From here, you can continue by a cable car to Zugspitz-Westgipfel Station, located at 2,950 meters with an amazing panoramic restaurant.

Zugspitz-Westgipfel Station

A highpoint of this journey is the opportunity to walk through a tunnel that is 800 meters long, complete with windows for viewing, to the top of the Bavarian cog railroad, the Schneefernerhaus station, where you will be able to ascent the viewing platforms at the eastern summit.

Schneefernerhaus Station

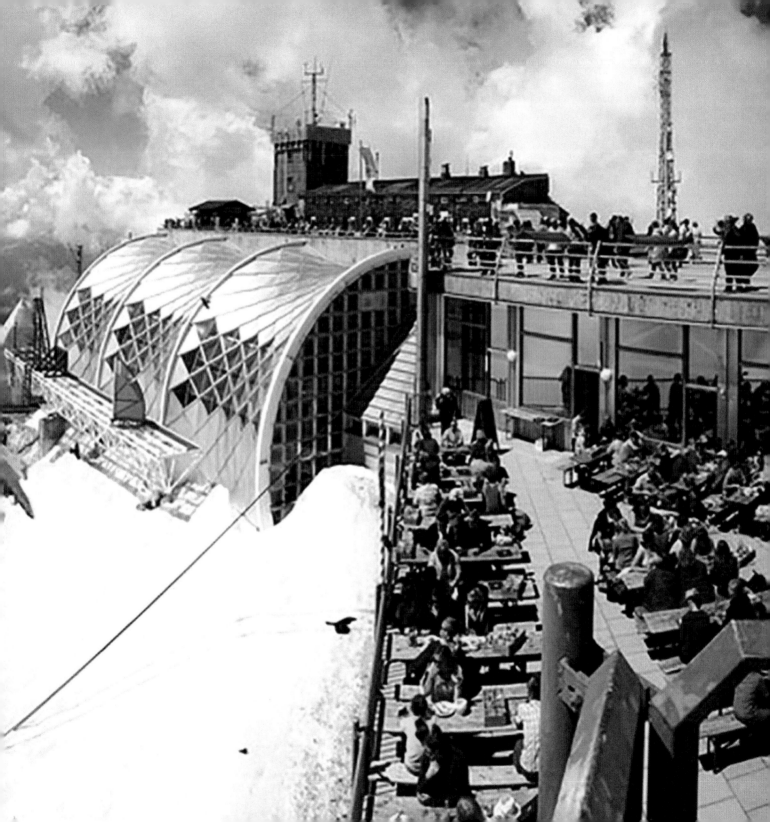

GERMANY
★ ★ ★

THE ISLAND OF RÜGEN

The most beautiful and largest of the German Baltic islands, Rügen is separated by the Strelasund from the mainland and links by a causeway to Stralsund, the mainland town. Its beauty stems from its diverse landscape that includes everything from expansive sandy beaches, lovely peninsulas to forest-covered hills and flat farmland.

Königsstuhl

GERMANY
★ ★ ★

Highlights of your visit might include the Subnitz beech forests that come to an end on the Königsstuhl where a sheer chalk cliff plummets down to the sea from 117 meters, as well as the Jasmund Peninsula that reaches heights of 161 meters. There is also an old, tiny resort town that you may want to visit, Putbus, where you will find several Neoclassical parks and buildings.

GERMANY
★ ★ ★

KÖNIGSSEE

Also referred to as King's Lake, this beautiful Bavarian lake is one of the terrific beauty areas located in the region known as Berchtesgadener Land. The Königssee is a paradise for walkers and is located near Salzburg. The footpath along the east side towards the Malerwinkel, also known as Painters' Corner, is one of the more popular routes, having superb views of the mountains and the lake.

Chapel of St. Bartholomew

In addition, you may want to take a boat trip to the Pilgrimage Chapel of St. Bartholomew from the 17th century located at the south end of the lake, where you can then take a walk to the Obersee. At the end of the Deutsche Alpenstrasse, Berchtesgaden is probably the most well-known tourist town as well as being one of the more popular mountain resorts located in the Bavarian Alps.

GERMANY
★ ★ ★

THE BERLIN WALL

While it may not be the most picturesque place to visit, what's left of the Berlin Wall is an attraction that you must visit when you are in Berlin, only so you can say that you have been there. The Wall was constructed in 1961 and was the more visible manifestation of the mentality of the Cold War that took place after World War II.

By the time it was taken down in 1990, it extended approximately 155 kilometers. Thankfully, the only remains of the wall that are still in existence are small sections that are covered with graffiti, which are stark reminders of the over 70 people that died as they attempted escape from the East.

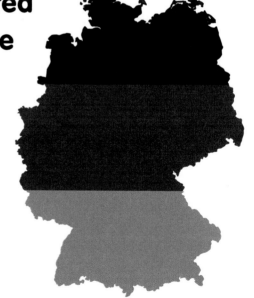

Berlin Central Station

Sections of the wall that are preserved include a stretch at the infamous Checkpoint Charlie, and a section opposite the Reichstag Building, known as Humboldthafen, where the names of all the victims are listed on the wall.

In addition, the Berlin Wall Exhibition is an excellent attraction, consisting of permanent exhibits that relate to the Berlin Wall, as well as the Berlin Wall Memorial.

Germany is full of culture, history, and natural beauty. From small towns and historic cities to forests and mountains, there is something to be enjoyed by all.

For additional information about Germany, you can visit your local library, research the internet, and ask questions of your teachers, family and friends.

Made in the USA
Coppell, TX
26 October 2021